beginner's guide to
sculpture

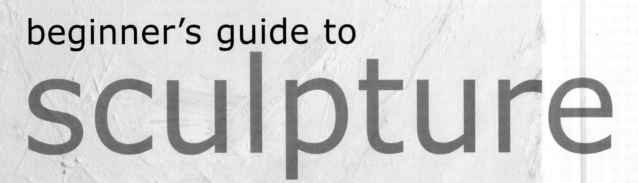

beginner's guide to
sculpture

Chloe Leaper

Published by SILVERDALE BOOKS
An imprint of Bookmart Ltd

Registered number 2372865

Trading as Bookmart Ltd
Desford Road
Enderby
Leicester LE19 4AD

© 2003 D&S Books Ltd

D&S Books Ltd
Kerswell,
Parkham Ash, Bideford
Devon, England
EX39 5PR

e-mail us at:-
enquiries@dsbooks.fsnet.co.uk

This edition printed 2003

ISBN 1-856056-84-8

Creative Director: Sarah King
Editor: Clare Haworth-Maden
Project Editor: Yvonne Worth
Photographer: Paul Forrester
Designer: Axis Design Editions Ltd

This book was created using Verdana

Printed in China

1 3 5 7 9 10 8 6 4 2

contents

introduction

The dictionary definitions of sculpture describe an art form that creates representations of existing objects through such materials as stone, clay, wood or metal casts. Sculpture is, however, the most diverse and evolving artistic medium. In addition, it is the only art form to deal directly with real space and, as such, has a close affinity with architecture, with its masses and planes of infinite intersections and varieties of view. This produces a special relationship with both creator and viewer.

There are four traditional methods of creating a sculpture: carving, modelling, casting and construction (an exclusively twentieth-century technique). In this book we shall be looking at these main methods of working in order to lay the foundations of a three-dimensional language with which we can develop our awareness of space, mass and weight, as well as our relationship with them.

In order to recreate a shape or form, we must first have an understanding of the structure of the subject, and before beginning a sculpture artists prepare themselves in many different ways. Drawing is a medium that is common to all visual artists, both as a medium in itself and as the most useful preparatory and research tool. We can use the medium of drawing to take visual notes of colour, texture, line and form, together with any feelings that we may have for the subject that we are studying. (If you do not wish to draw, however, spending at least five minutes examining and really questioning how forms feel, weigh and look in space will unconsciously help your future creation processes.) Most artists use drawing as a way of

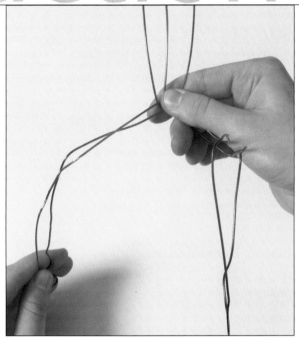

A WIRE ARMATURE ACTS AS A SKELETON TO INTERNALLY SUPPORT YOUR SCULPTURE.

SKETCHING IS A VERY IMPORTANT TOOL IN THE PRELIMINARY STAGES OF A SCULPTURE DESIGN.

gaining insight into, and building a relationship with, the form that they wish to recreate and express. With more complicated sculptures, and particularly for carvings, when the smallest mistake can be irrevocably costly, the artist may sometimes start by making a smaller scale model called a maquette.

a brief history of sculpture

FOR MANY CENTURIES SCULPTURES WERE CREATED TO REFLECT THE SPIRITUAL BELIEFS OF THOSE WHO CREATED THEM. THESE RANGE FROM THE ANCIENT EGYPTIANS, WHOSE MAJESTIC SPHINX (TOP) IS PROBABLY ONE OF THE WORLD'S BEST KNOWN IMAGES, TO THE ORNATE CARVINGS AND STATUARY FOUND IN CHRISTIAN CHURCHES (ABOVE).

Early sculpture dates back to 30,000 bc, with works ranging from decorated pottery to ritualistic figurines and symbolic charms. From ancient to medieval times, sculptures were created for religious, mythological or spiritual purposes as reflections of humankind's various belief systems. The style of this subject matter ranged from the numerous naïve medieval carvings of the Madonna and Child to the intricate technical mastery of baroque altarpieces.

It was not until the seventeenth century and the birth of realism that artists turned to real life for their subject matter. Art came to be considered as a separate entity, questioning our relationship with the world and our consequent representation of it. As realism became established, such artists as Claude Monet (1840–1926) and Edgar Degas (1834–1917) began to move away from traditional realism and, instead, produced impressions of what they saw. Impressionism, as it was known, developed into expressionism, with an even more symbolic style. Then followed a major revolution in art, led by such cubists as Pablo Picasso (1881–1973), who made abstracts of traditional subjects, using every view of the objects in a single sculpture to produce a holistic creation of objects in space.

new sculpting
materials and techniques

MODERN SCULPTING METHODS TODAY INCORPORATE A WIDE RANGE OF TECHNIQUES AND MATERIALS, INCLUDING VIDEO, FILM AND COMPUTER MODELLING.

The rapid development of scientific and industrial research during the twentieth and twenty-first centuries has brought about the increasing availability of new materials and techniques. Modern techniques that deal with metals, in particular steel, have given sculptors the opportunity to work on much heavier, gravity-defying constructions than before, which make full use of the new joining and lifting techniques. The development of plastics has also opened up the relationship between the internal and external space of a sculpture. With the traditional restrictions having been removed, sculptors have been able to enjoy a new and exciting relationship with space and mass, as well as with movement and light.

Technological advancements have also brought video and film into the domain of sculpture, and many sculptors today choose a much more diverse sculpting practice than was available to their predecessors.

materials and equipment

materials

materials

More than any other art medium, sculpture requires a special understanding of, and excitement for, materials. The basic techniques and principles of carving, modelling and metal-casting in use today have not changed from the days when they were employed by ancient civilisations. The greatest sculptors have been those who have had respect for, and an appreciation of, the inherent qualities of their materials. These materials can be as diverse as stone, clay, plaster, metal, paper, soap and even glitter. There are never any rules as to what is acceptable as a material, and there are always alternatives should you not be able to find the materials advocated in the projects in this book.

IT IS IMPORTANT TO MIX YOUR CLAY THOROUGHLY, USING THE WEDGING TECHNIQUE (SEE PAGE 13).

▶ ▶

CONSTRUCT YOUR OWN PLASTER-CASTING
MOULDS OUT OF WOOD.

The main materials with which we shall be working that require some degree of technical tutoring are clay and plaster. For this reason it is important to read these sections (see pages 13–14 and 15–16) before starting on any of the projects that use these materials.

you will need the following materials

four pieces of wood
    measuring 2 x 1 x 25cm
    (around 1 x ½ x 10 in)
clay (traditional or synthetic)
plaster
black, white, red, blue and
    silver acrylic or emulsion paint
muslin (or a similarly very thin fabric)
3 mm (^{2}/₁₆ in) wire
sheet metal (or metallic card)
red, silver and bronze spray paint
glitter
paper and card
a balloon
PVA glue
newspaper
soap
assemblage items
latex solution
photos
a sketchbook
wire

BE ADVENTUROUS IN YOUR CHOICE OF MATERIALS – ANYTHING GOES!

INVEST IN A ROLL OF 3 MM (2/16 IN) WIRE, AS IT IS USEFUL FOR ARMATURES AND CONSTRUCTION.

tools and equipment

Most of the tools that are needed to carry out these projects will probably already be lying in most households' kitchens and toolboxes, and any other tools should be readily available from hardware shops or art suppliers. However, because I believe that sculpture should always be accessible, and shouldn't require the purchase of expensive tools, I will always suggest alternative ways of using the tools that you may already have.

IF YOU DO NOT HAVE THE EXACT TOOLS OR MATERIALS – IMPROVISE! USE A KNIFE INSTEAD OF SCISSORS, OR DRAIN-PIPING INSTEAD OF A ROLLING PIN.

you will need the following tools

a rolling pin
  (or length of cylindrical tubing)
2 roller guides
  (or two pieces of wood 1 cm (½ in)
  thick and 50 cm (19 in) long), or
  poster frames
paper and pencils
scissors (or a scalpel)
small, medium and large paintbrushes
serrated blade
Vaseline petroleum jelly
  (or vegetable oil or fat)
wire cutters (or strong scissors)
wire pincers (or tweezers)
metal cutters (or strong scissors)
a marker pen
a hammer
a disposable plastic cup
masking tape (or sticky tape)
a screwdriver
eight screws
a plastic bowl
clingfilm
a toothbrush
glue or a glue gun
a selection of clay-working tools
  (or spoons, forks and knives)
file or sandpaper
a drill and drill bit
wax

clay preparation and care

Clay was traditionally dug directly from the earth and then modelled into shape before being fired at a high temperature to strengthen it and make permanent forms that can last for thousands of years. However, in order to work with traditional clays – ranging from porcelain through terracotta to crank – you must have access to a kiln. Although community colleges that offer evening classes in ceramics often allow people to fire work in their kilns, so many synthetic clays (which can either be fired in a kitchen cooker or simply left to dry) are now available from most art suppliers that there is no longer any need to undertake the problematic process of firing traditional clay.

Because clay dries out very easily, it should always be stored in an airtight container or bag. If your clay does dry out, however, simply break it up into small pieces, add about an equal volume of water and the clay will then reconstitute itself. Before using reconstituted clay, spend at least five minutes cutting the block of clay in half and then slamming the halves back together again, alternately cutting the clay vertically and horizontally as you repeat the process (which is called 'wedging' and ensures that no air bubbles remain within the clay).

wedging

   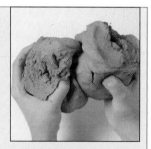

IF THE CLAY HAS BEEN RECONSTITUTED FROM LEFTOVER PIECES, IT IS IMPORTANT TO MIX IT THOROUGHLY BEFORE YOU BEGIN.

KNEAD THE CLAY INTO A SAUSAGE SHAPE, THEN TWIST THE CLAY UNTIL IT SEPARATES IN HALF.

YOU WILL BE ABLE TO SEE THE AIR BUBBLES AND GAPS WHERE ALL THE LEFTOVER PIECES HAVE BEEN PUSHED TOGETHER.

SLAM THE TWO HALVES TOGETHER FIRMLY, THEN KNEAD INTO A SAUSAGE SHAPE AND REPEAT THE PROCESS.

materials

In order to learn about joining clay, you must first make a slip pot. Do this by making a fist-sized ball of clay, sticking your thumb in the centre so that you create a hollow, bowl shape, adding a little water and then stirring it with a paintbrush until a slip is formed that is the consistency of thick double cream. This slip acts as a bond between two pieces of clay and will make your joins melt into one another.

making a slip pot

BEGIN BY TAKING A
SMALL LUMP OF CLAY
AND MODELLING IT INTO
A BALL.

STICK YOUR THUMB INTO
THE CENTRE OF THE
BALL.

PINCH YOUR THUMB AND
FINGERS TOGETHER TO
EASE OUT A BOWL
SHAPE.

POUR A LITTLE WATER
INTO THE HOLLOW OF
YOUR POT.

STIR THE WATER WITH A
PAINTBRUSH. THE WATER
WILL GRADUALLY MIX
WITH THE CLAY.

WHEN MIXED WITH
ENOUGH CLAY IT WILL
FORM A 'SLIP' – WITH
THE CONSISTENCY OF
WHIPPED CREAM.

plaster preparation
and care ▶▶

Plaster is most commonly used for replication purposes, such as the reproduction of Greek and Roman statues. Plaster can, however, be used as a material in its own right: when cast into a block, for instance, it makes a cheaper alternative to stone that is also much easier to carve. Because it reacts over time with the moisture in the air, causing it to set and become hard, plaster should be kept in an airtight container and stored in a dry place.

When mixing plaster, first half-fill a suitable plastic bowl with water. Then begin to sprinkle the plaster evenly over the surface of the water until a peak forms in the centre. Next, mix the plaster with your hand until all of the lumps have disappeared and the mixture has the consistency of double cream. Before pouring the plaster mixture into a mould, tap the bowl on the table so that all of the air bubbles rise to the surface to ensure that when the plaster sets and is removed from the mould it will contain no air holes. Mixing plaster creates a chemical reaction, and if you want to speed up this drying reaction, use warmer water, while if you want to slow it down, use colder water. Never, however, change the

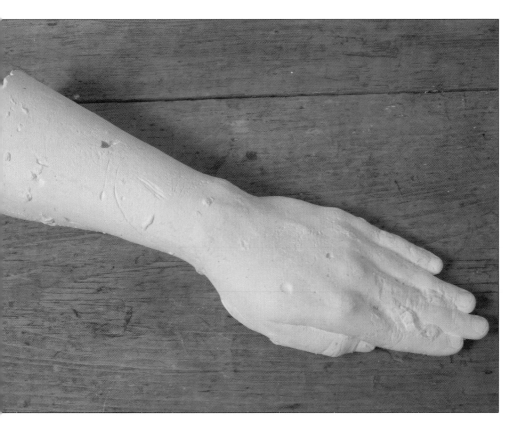

THIS PIECE IMITATES THE CAST RELICS OF ANCIENT GREECE.

materials

plaster-to-water ratio because this will only result in poor plaster
that crumbles easily. As plaster sets it releases heat, so when
your plaster is cold and dry you will know that it has set
completely.

mixing plaster

HALF FILL A SMALL
MIXING CONTAINER WITH
WATER, THEN TAKE A
HANDFUL OF PLASTER
AND SPRINKLE IT OVER
THE SURFACE, TAKING
CARE TO SQUEEZE OUT
ANY LUMPS.

KEEP SPRINKLING UNTIL
A PEAK OF PLASTER
BEGINS TO FORM ON
THE SURFACE.

MIX THE PLASTER
THOROUGHLY WITH YOUR
HAND, REMOVING ANY
LUMPS.

THE PLASTER SHOULD BE
THE CONSISTENCY OF
DOUBLE CREAM.

HEALTH AND SAFETY

There are a few basic rules to which you should adhere when working on these projects.

- When using plaster, dry clay or spray paint, always wear a dust or respiratory mask and work in a well-ventilated area
- When clipping plaster, always wear goggles.
- When bending sharp wire, cutting with a scalpel or hammering metal, always wear protective gloves.
- Always wash your hands thoroughly after using glue, paint or plaster.

basic
techniques

modelling

The process of modelling is one in which the form is built up using a malleable material, such as clay or wax, which gives the sculptor much greater freedom because one can add or subtract material to the form, enabling any mistakes to be amended or rebuilt.

When modelling a large form, the sculptor may sometimes create an armature, a rigid, internal skeleton (usually made of wood or metal) that helps to support the malleable material if it cannot bear its own weight. The armature's form must, of course, itself be carefully considered because it will strongly determine the form of the finished sculpture. Another important consideration when modelling is surface texture because it is important to take advantage of the pliability of the materials with which you are working. Modelling provides the sculptor with a more direct and spontaneous form of expression than carving or construction and is usually the route into the medium for most sculptors.

The projects in this section (see pages 25 to 60) use clay, papier-mâché and plaster to demonstrate modelling's potential breadth. In the clay projects, we shall look at three basic methods of using clay: slabwork, direct modelling and modelling by assembling parts.

MODEL AROUND AN ARMATURE FOR EXTRA INTERNAL SUPPORT.

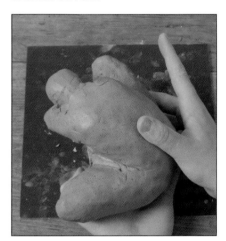

YOUR HANDS ARE YOUR BEST TOOLS WHEN MODELLING.

JOINING CAREFULLY IS ESPECIALLY IMPORTANT WHEN MODELLING WITH CLAY.

MODELLING IS THE OLDEST METHOD OF SCULPTING.

carving

YOU CAN CARVE A WIDE VARIETY OF MATERIALS OTHER THAN STONE.

IMITATING RELIEF CARVING IS FAR LESS TIME-CONSUMING AND JUST AS EFFECTIVE.

THE IMPOSING GRANDEUR OF THE EASTER ISLAND CARVED STATUES ARE PRIMITIVE, YET ARRESTING.

Carving is essentially a subtractive process whereby the sculptor chisels, cuts and chips the outer surface of a solid block of wood or stone to varying depths in order to create a sculpture. Carvings were traditionally created from stone, such as marble, granite, limestone and sandstone. These materials, particularly marble, are extremely hard and require a great degree of patience to sculpt (during the Renaissance period, a life-sized sculpture of a person would take many years to carve). Because it relies on extensive planning and technical ability, carving is perhaps the most difficult and laborious way of creating a sculpture, and if you make a mistake whilst carving, you cannot return what you have taken away.

There are two traditional approaches to, or styles of, carving. One approach uses a 'relief' method to create shallowly carved sculptures, which often take the form of plaques depicting stories or symbolic icons. This style involves a careful consideration of the use of perspective and contrasts in depth. The second way of carving focuses on creating a completely three-dimensional sculpture that considers all aspects and views of the sculpture. There are also two ways of viewing and treating carving as a sculptor. You can either find the form within, and by this I mean letting the material itself guide the form that you carve, or you can impose your own form directly onto the material and not be guided by its natural shape and textures. Both approaches are valid, although I believe that even when imposing a shape onto a block of wood, stone or plaster you should always be aware of, and accommodate, the natural characteristics of your material.

casting
techniques

Casting was traditionally used solely as a method of reproducing or mass-producing existing sculptures in a more permanent material, transforming, for example, a wax sculpture into bronze or one of unfired clay into plaster. The two traditional sculpting techniques that use casting are, firstly, the lost-wax method for casting bronze and, secondly, sand casting.

The lost-wax process involves making a sculpture in wax, which is then covered in plaster. This is fired at a high temperature so that the wax melts and runs out, leaving a hollow, negative cavity where the original wax sculpture once was. Molten bronze is then poured into the plaster and left to set, after which the plaster is chipped off, leaving an exact bronze replica of the original wax sculpture. Small models may be cast as solid sculptures, but larger ones usually require a more complicated casting process. Sand-casting involves making negative, imprinted sections of the outside of the chosen object and then reassembling the segments and pouring in plaster to produce an identical version of the original object.

In the section on casting (see pages 73 to 86), we will be looking at different, and more manageable, ways of casting. We will be using latex to create flexible moulds that do not require any segments and will cast a replica of an arm using an interesting plaster technique. We will also use the traditional relief-casting technique of imprinting and casting into clay.

CONSIDER UNDERCUTS WHEN CASTING, TO ENSURE EASY REMOVAL OF THE OBJECT.

LATEX IS FLEXIBLE AND WILL NOT DAMAGE THE CAST OBJECT.

CASTING TECHNIQUES FOR METALS ARE NOT RESTRICTED TO SMALL MODELS — SOME ARE HUGE UNDERTAKINGS LIKE THIS BUDDHA.

construction

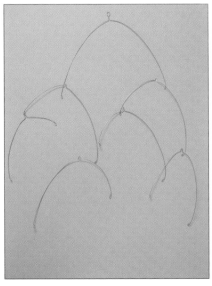

THE CONSTRUCTION METHOD ALLOWS THE WIDEST RANGE OF MATERIALS IN SCULPTURE PRACTICE.

Construction, a technique that dates from the twentieth century, involves building a sculpture from various component parts, be they of the same or different materials. Construction is largely the result of new industrial research and techniques that allow sculptors to work on a much bigger scale than before, irrespective of gravitational constraints. New materials, such as steel, sheet glass, fibreglass, aluminium, latex, plastics, resins, concrete and many others, have given the sculptor a huge range of exciting tactile possibilities. Construction was developed from assemblage art, whereby a sculptor collects and assembles objects and found objects (essentially rubbish) into new sculptural forms. Some of the first examples of this type of work were created by Picasso,

CONSTRUCTION ENCOMPASSES TECHNIQUES RANGING FROM WELDING TO USING GLUE GUNS!

techniques

who assembled a bike seat and handlebars in the form of a bull's head.

The projects in this section (see pages 87 to 107) will take you through the use of a variety of non-traditional materials, such as metal wire, mirror card and found objects, as well as various ways of making sculptures from them. This section offers the most diverse approach to sculpture, encouraging your imagination to roam freely to enable you to discover new ways of making forms and structures.

BE IMAGINATIVE WITH THE FORMS, MATERIALS AND TECHNIQUES YOU USE TO CONSTRUCT.

CONSTRUCTION TECHNIQUES CAN PROVIDE GREAT FREEDOM OF CHOICE FOR ARTISTS — AS WELL AS SOME FUN!

the projects

the projects

The projects in this book have been designed to familiarize you with the basic materials, techniques and concepts of sculpting. Each project tackles one particular aspect or technique of the four main forms of sculpture: carving, casting, modelling and construction.

The projects should be regarded as outlines so that you feel able to evolve and develop them in any direction that interests you. Remember to have fun, and never be afraid to adapt or edit a project where you see fit!

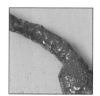

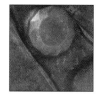

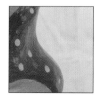

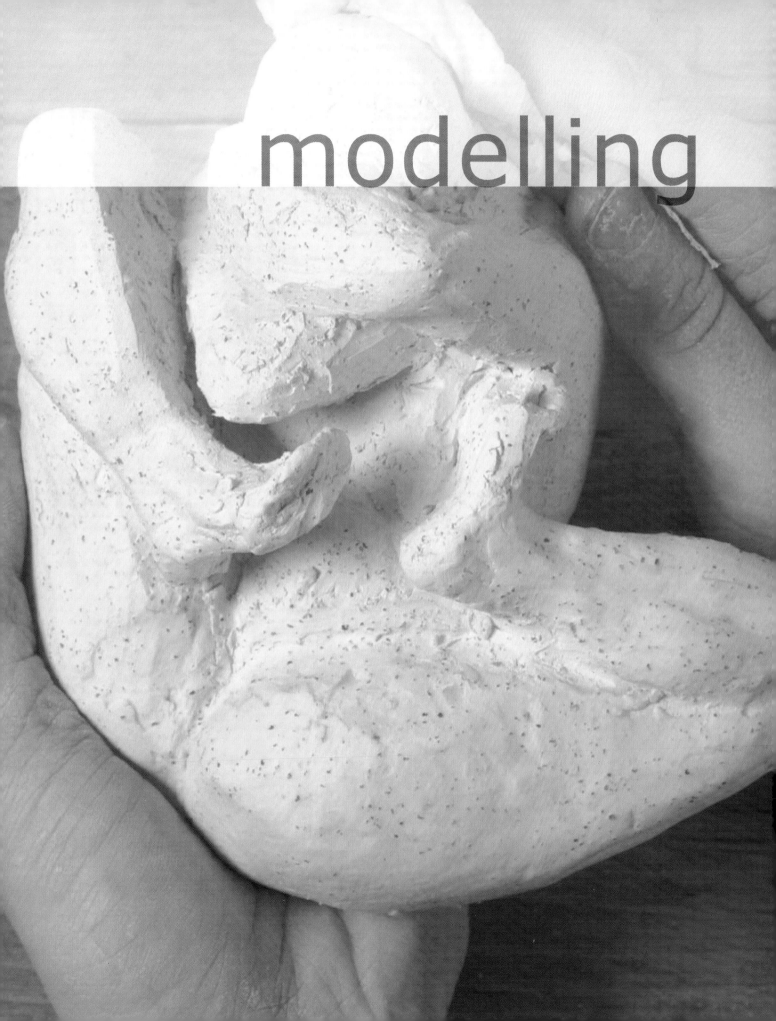

modelling

clay-ball figure

ball

you will need

clay

clay-working tools

slip pot and paintbrush

wax

natural varnish

a cloth

The human figure has been the primary subject for all artistic disciplines throughout the history of art, only losing its precedence slightly during the twentieth century. Clay representations of the human figure, which were used for such rituals as fertility rites, date back to prehistoric times, when the forms were symbolic, the only distinguishing features being typically breasts and stomachs. Over the following centuries, these simplistic, sculptural representations became more and more refined until, by the Renaissance period, they were almost exact replicas of the human form. During the last century, there has been a shift back to simplistic abstraction: it is not necessary to labour over detail when you can capture the essence and impression of a figure instead.

It is fundamental, however, that all sculptors learn to capture and express the wonderful form that is the human figure. As well as helping you to get a feel for the human figure, this project will teach you some basic methods of working with clay in an expressive and flexible manner. Because the historical relationship between claywork and the human figure inclines me towards a natural finish, you will not be required to create any complicated ones.

I will also introduce you to some basic clay-working tools, which are usually made of wood and have two different ends with which to produce different markings. It is not necessary to spend a great deal of money on new tools, however, and a knife will be adequate for all of the clay projects.

ball

1 Having made some preliminary sketches or taken some photographs of curled-up figures, choose the pose that you find the most interesting.

2 Study your chosen pose and then divide it into leg, body, arm and head sections. Working section by section, make the basic segments for the legs, head, body and arms.

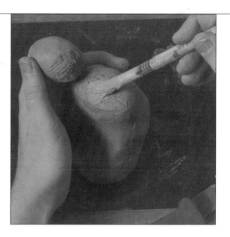

3 Using a knife, roughen the surfaces where the base of the head meets the top of the body, add slip to the rough areas and push the head onto the body.

4 Using a tool, blend the head with the body, pressing the clay together at the join until you have made a smooth connection. Blending is important because it smoothes out any air bubbles, which, if the clay is then fired, may break the join.

5 Next, roughen the ends of the legs and the area of the body to which they will be joined.

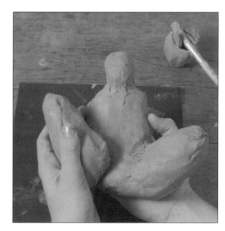

6 Again paint on some slip and then blend the joins carefully so that the legs are firmly and securely positioned.

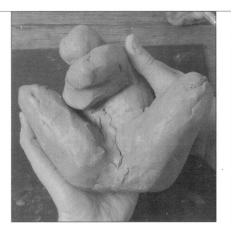

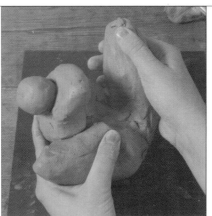

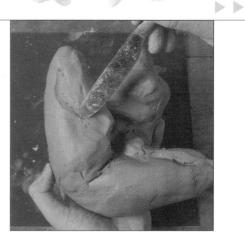

7 Repeat steps 4, 5 and 6 for the arms.

8 Now that you have constructed the basic shape, you can spend some time finalising the position and begin shaping the figure more accurately.

9 Take a pointed tool and start to define the creases in the legs. You should start forming the feet at this point, too.

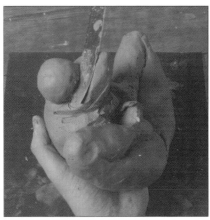

10 Using a knife, mould the basic structure of the feet, which are made up of a series of planes. Use the knife to give some muscle definition to the legs as well.

11 Begin working on the arms, using the same processes as for the feet and legs (see steps 8, 9 and 10).

12 Now you are ready to begin work on the body and head. We will not sculpt any facial details on this sculpture because I am aiming to convey only the essence of the human form.

ball

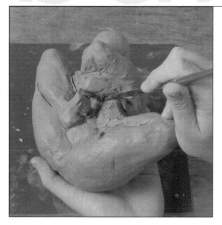

13 Concentrate now on the breasts and stomach (the emphasised features of ancient sculptures), using a pointed tool to define these areas.

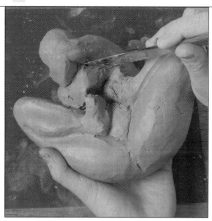

14 Now that the sculpture is essentially finished, use a pointed tool to clean up all of the lines, especially those in the more detailed areas.

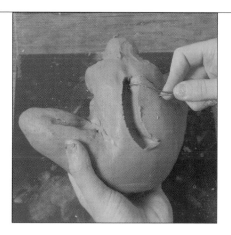

15 If you are working in traditional clay, you must now hollow out the sculpture (even if you are using synthetic clay, this is still good practice). Start by taking a wire-loop tool and beginning to scoop out the bulk of the clay from the back.

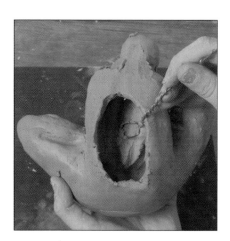

16 While hollowing, take care not to puncture through to the outside.

17 Mould a flat piece of clay large enough to cover the hole. Roughen the edge of the hole and the edge of the covering clay.

18 Add some slip to the rough areas and then gently push the covering clay over the hole.

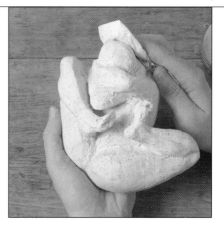

19 Carefully blend the edges of the covering clay so that the back looks smooth. If you have a rubber kidney tool, gently tap the figure into shape (alternatively, use a wooden spoon). If it is to be fired, take a pointed tool and push it all the way into the centre of the sculpture (this hole will prevent the piece from exploding).

20 When the piece is dry or fired, depending on whether you use synthetic or real clay, take a knife tool and finish off the sculpture. Then, using a cloth, rub some natural varnish into the clay.

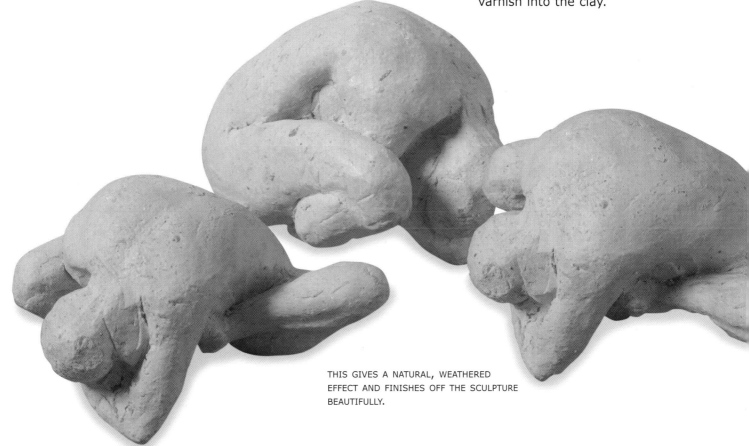

THIS GIVES A NATURAL, WEATHERED EFFECT AND FINISHES OFF THE SCULPTURE BEAUTIFULLY.

acrobat

you will need

250 cm (98 in) wire or longer
wire cutters and pincers
masking or sticky tape
newspaper or tissue paper
plaster, water and a plastic
    bowl
different-sized strips of muslin
    or a thin fabric
glossy spray paint in a bright
    dynamic colour, such as
    red, yellow, orange or
    any bright metallic colour
PVA glue
glitter
invisible thread

This project aims to capture movement using the expressive quality of modelling. I started by drawing and studying acrobats and dancers from life and also by looking at magazine photographs, which often capture the hard-to-draw movements of people in motion. I arranged a lay figure into various acrobatic positions, too, until I decided upon a final pose. Although it is not necessary to use either drawings or a lay figure when preparing to make the sculpture, it is important to study the human anatomy by looking at photographs and to be aware of what a human body can, and can't, do. If you wish to draw from life, you may be able to arrange to study human motion by attending local gym and dance groups.

As well as learning about capturing physical movement in sculpture, we will look at how surface effects can add movement. Although it is not a traditional material, we will use glitter because it sparkles and reflects the light, giving a sense of movement and animation. (Sculptors have increasingly used unusual materials like glitter over the last forty years for their kitsch, or child-like, properties.) We will also use a strong, vibrant colour, such as red, whose naturally dynamic properties will add to the effect of movement that we hope to capture.

In order literally to give our sculpture movement, we will display it by hanging it from invisible wire so that it will float and rotate in the air. It is always important to consider how to display a sculpture to do it justice when viewed from every angle, particularly when dealing with a three-dimensional piece.

This project has furthermore been designed to teach you the basic principles of armature-making, along with an appreciation of how an armature supports and dictates the final form. It will teach you how to design a strong, uncomplicated armature with minimal joins (the more joins an armature has, the weaker it will be).

acrobat

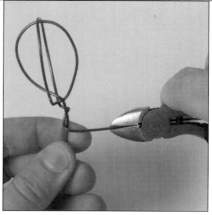

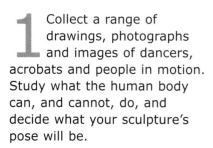

1 Collect a range of drawings, photographs and images of dancers, acrobats and people in motion. Study what the human body can, and cannot, do, and decide what your sculpture's pose will be.

2 When you have decided on a pose that is fluid and full of movement, such as this, position a lay figure, or make a sketch of the pose that you have chosen and place it in front of you, so that you can continually refer to it as you are working.

3 In order to make the wire armature, you will need a roll of wire. We will begin at the head. Bend the end of the wire at a right angle for the neck, following through to make a complete circle, which will be the silhouette of the head from the front. Instead of joining the end of the circle to the right-angle corner, create another circle, which will be the silhouette of the head from the side. Tie the wire around the 'neck' and bend it to the left to create the left shoulder, then take the wire down and back up again to create the left arm.

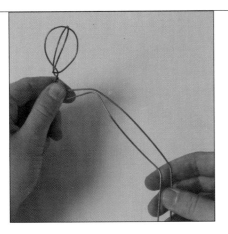

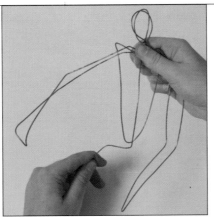

4 Having returned the end of the wire to the neck, bend it to the right to create the right shoulder and then take it down and back up again to create the right arm.

5 In the same way as you did for the head, bend the wire into a silhouette of the body from the front, again ending at the neck.

6 As you did for the arms, bend the wire down and then up again to create the left leg before taking it across to the right to make the pelvic bone. Repeat for the right leg and then finish off the armature by wrapping the wire around the waist a couple of times.

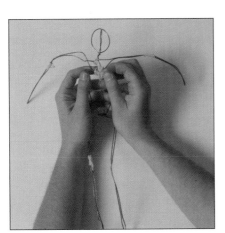

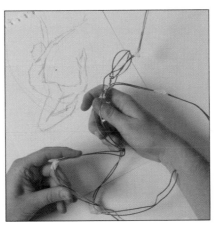

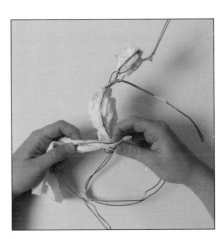

7 Now take some masking or sticky tape and tape it around the neck, shoulders, waist and pelvic edge.

8 Referring to your lay figure or drawing, bend the wire frame into your preferred position.

9 Fill the head, body, arm and leg cavities with some crumpled newspaper or tissue paper, taping in the paper as you go.

acrobat

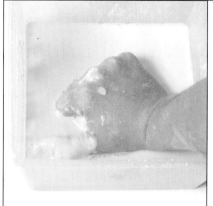

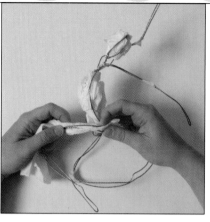

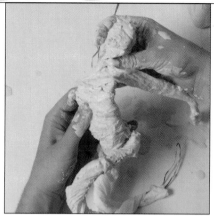

10 Now mix up a bowl of plaster (see page 16).

11 Place some small strips of thin fabric (like muslin or even strong kitchen paper) in the plaster bowl and then mix the contents until all of the fabric is covered with plaster. (Although you could use plaster-impregnated bandages, it is cheaper and just as effective to make your own.

12 Fish out some smaller strips of plaster-covered fabric and wrap them around the head. Because plaster dries very quickly, smooth the surface as you work to prevent your sculpture from becoming too bumpy. Wrap larger strips of plaster-covered fabric around the body, paying particular attention to the areas where the legs, arms and head join.

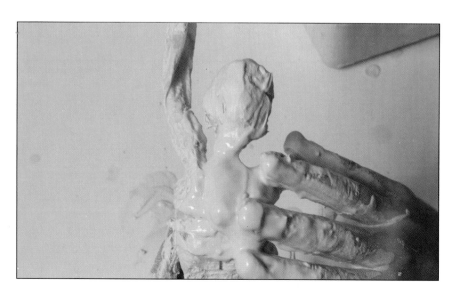

13 When you have completely covered the wire frame in this way, rub a thin layer of plaster all over the figure to provide a smoother finish (don't overdo it though because a rough surface catches the light and gives a greater sense of movement).

14 Now leave the sculpture to dry.

15 When the sculpture is dry, spray it with a glossy spray paint (making sure that your workspace is well ventilated) and then leave it to dry again.

16 When the paint has dried, cover the sculpture with a thin layer of PVA glue and then sprinkle glitter over the entire figure. (Doing this over a sheet of paper will enable you to pour any glitter that falls off back into the pot to use again.) Then leave the sculpture to dry.

17 Take some invisible thread and loop it around the arms of the sculpture. Select a place that catches the light and then hang your sculpture there so that it is free to move and sparkle.

slabwork horse ►►

you will need

clay

a rolling pin

two roller guides

    measuring 1 cm (½ in)

    in depth

clay-working tools

cardboard tubing

    measuring 20 cm (8 in)

    in length

paper and pencil

scissors

a hard brush,

    such as a toothbrush

paintbrushes

white paint

black gloss paint

In this project we shall be focusing on one of the most useful techniques when working in clay: slabwork, which consists of constructing a sculpture by joining slabs of clay together. This method enables the sculptor to produce much larger, self-supporting sculptures than modelling does. Although some sculptors use an external armature to support the sculpture as it dries, there is no need for a permanent internal armature.

When working with clay, it is advisable to do so on a rather rough surface – like a wooden chopping board – because the clay will stick to shiny surfaces, such as plastic or marble worktops. When making slabs, it is best to start with a fresh lump of clay, one that has come straight out of the bag, having already been thoroughly mixed by the manufacturer.

When creating a slabwork sculpture, the clay's consistency is very important: it should not be so hard as to crack when being rolled, but should not be sticky to the touch either. If it is too wet, expose it to the air for about ten minutes until it is moist and pliable and does not stick to the work surface. If it is too dry, sprinkle a little water over it and then mix the clay until it is suitably pliable.

Then, using the outer edge of your hand, begin to karate-chop the block of clay, working from the centre outwards until you have flattened it to a thickness of about 4 cm (1 in). Place two roller guides or lengths of wood about 1-2cm (½-1 in) thick either side of the clay and roll it out. Regularly flip the clay over to ensure that it doesn't stick to the work surface.

slabwork

1 Prepare a slab of clay (see page 40 for instructions) measuring around 30 x 30 cm (11 x 11 in).

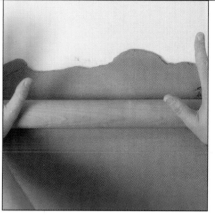

2 Using a rolling pin, roll out the clay to the same depth as the roller guides.

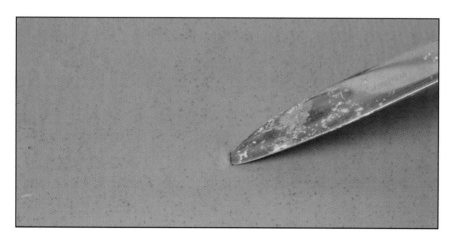

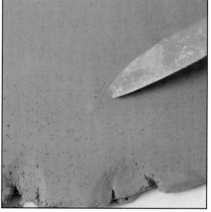

3 Take good care to remove any air holes and lumps, using a knife blade.

▶ ▶

4 Measure and cut a rectangle of clay 30 cm (11 in) long and 20 cm (8 in) wide.

5 Use the excess clay to make a slip pot (see page 14 for instructions), which you will need later when joining the slabs together.

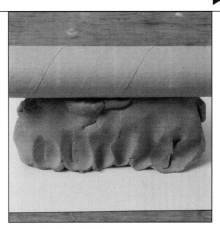

6 Next, take another lump of clay and mould it to support the length of cardboard tubing.

7 Lay the prepared slab of clay over the tube so that the ends of the slab touch the work surface on either side. This will be the body of the horse. Make sure that the slab is stable by adjusting the block of clay supporting the tube.

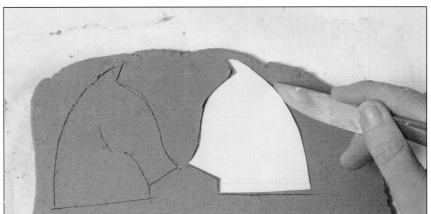

8 Now prepare, roll out and cut a new slab of clay measuring the same as the previous one (see steps 1, 2 and 3). Using a pencil and paper, draw a silhouette of a horse's head (my drawing gives an idea of what the head could look like). Cut out this drawing, place it over the new slab and cut around it. Then repeat this step so that you have two clay heads.

slabwork

9 Using a serrated tool, roughen the base of one of the heads.

10 Now roughen a patch of clay at one end of the horse's body, just to the side. Add some slip to the roughened areas and then push the head onto the body.

11 Using a flat-edged tool, smooth both sides of the head onto the body.

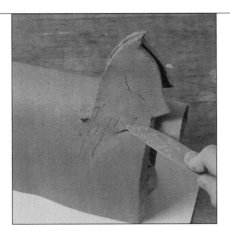

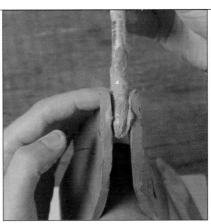

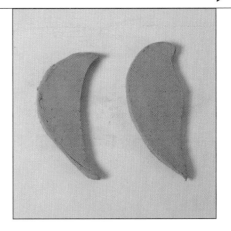

12
Repeat steps 7, 8 and 9 for the other head shape so that it is firmly joined to the body.

13
Paint some slip onto the point of contact where the two heads meet at the top and then gently push them together. Using a pointed tool, smooth the edges of the join together, taking care not to lose any of the ears' definition.

14
Return to your pencil and paper and draw the horse's tail and mane (my drawings may give you inspiration). Cut out these drawings, place them over your clay and cut around them so that you have one mane and one tail shape.

slabwork

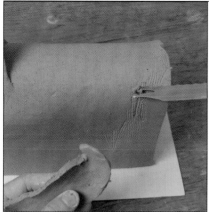  

15 Using a serrated tool, roughen the body end of the tail and the area of the body to which the tail will be attached.

16 Add some slip to the body end of the tail and then join it to the body so that it sweeps around the back end of the horse.

17 Using a serrated tool, roughen the edges of the mane. Do the same to the area of the head to which it will be joined. Add some slip to the roughened areas and then attach the mane to the head, sweeping it around the head in the opposite direction to the tail so that you will see the tail when viewing the sculpture from one side and the mane when viewing it from the other.

18 Leave the sculpture exposed to the air until the clay has reached the 'leather-hard' stage (when the clay has dried to the extent that it is almost rigid, but still a little damp). Using a serrated knife, scratch the surface of the horse's entire body.

19 Do not scratch the mane and tail, however, but instead smooth them with a flat tool (we shall use this contrast of rough and smooth to good effect in step 21).

20 Either leave the clay to dry out or, if you are working with traditional clay, fire it.

21 Using a hard brush, such as a toothbrush, paint the body and head of the horse white.

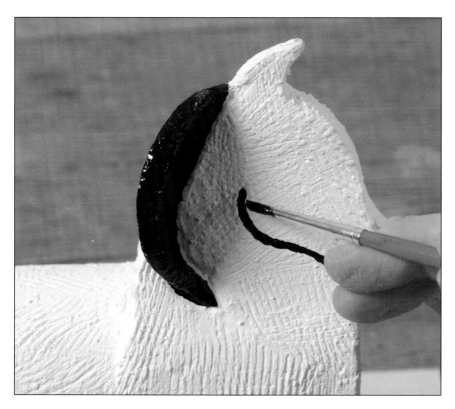

22 Paint the tail and mane with black gloss paint to highlight further the contrast of rough and smooth. (Although you could use any colours with which to paint your horse, I think that a black-and-white finish is sophisticated and simple.)

papier-mâché portrait ▸▸

portrait

you will need

- a balloon
- card and a pencil
- scissors
- sticky tape
- tissue paper
- paper
- a bowl, water and strips
    of newspaper
- PVA glue
- paintbrushes
- white, red, yellow,
    blue and black paints

Portraiture has been an enduring theme in sculpture for thousands of years, ranging from the 'mummy' coffins of ancient Egyptian kings through the highly coloured busts of Greek notaries and eminent philosophers to the marbles of the Renaissance and the abstract clay sculptures of contemporary artists. Almost all of the great sculptors over the years have either explored the theme of self-portraiture or have been commissioned to sculpt portraits of their patrons or friends.

In this project we will give a contemporary twist to portraiture and will try to move away from some of the traditional preconceptions that surround it. Firstly, although sculptural portraits were traditionally made out of such durable materials as marble or bronze to act as enduring memorials to their subjects, we will be using papier-mâché, a light-weight, non-durable material that enables more flexibility when sculpting. Secondly, although it is traditionally the norm for portraits to be the colour of the material that was used to make them, such as brown in the case of bronze or white in that of marble, it is commonly thought that the ancient Greek marble sculptures that today appear purely white were actually brightly painted when they were first made. For this reason, we will be painting our sculpture, using exaggerated colour tones and highlighting and darkening the skin and hair tones for extra effect. We will also accentuate the main features in the way one would a caricature, giving the portrait a slightly cartoon-like look and thereby adding to the sculpture's contemporary feel.

To make your basic glue solution, mix about three tablespoons of PVA glue into a medium-sized bowl of water. Tear strips of newspaper and allow them to soak in the solution for at least five minutes before using.

portrait

1 Inflate a balloon and then tie the end. This will act as an armature for your sculpture and will form the basic shape of the head.

2 Next, place the balloon in the middle of a sheet of card and, using a pencil, draw around the bottom half of the balloon. This curved line will form the top of the neck and the balloon will be attached to it. Imagining that the curved line is the line of the chin, draw a neck with a flat bottom. Starting from the centre of the line of the chin, then draw a line halfway down the neck.

3 Cut out the neck support and then make another as described in step 2, but this time draw a line from the bottom of the neck up to the centre of the line of the chin. Cut down both lines and then slot the two neck supports together so that they form one support when standing up.

4 Using sticky tape, attach the balloon to the neck support.

▶ ▶

5 Now draw the silhouette of your subject's face from the side, working from your drawing, photograph or your subject him- or herself. (The drawing will give your sculpture an authentic structure and does not have to be exact.)

6 Cut out the profile with a curved right-hand edge to enable you to stick the profile to the balloon. Using sticky tape, fix the profile to the balloon.

7 Although the card provides the basic profile shape when viewed from the side, you'll need to bulk out the nose for the front view, so crumple up some tissue paper so that it forms the shape of your subject's nose and then attach it to the profile.

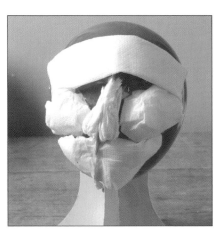

8 Using more tissue paper, make cheek, chin and brow shapes and then fix them onto the head to form its basic structure.

9 Fold a square of paper in such a way that it eventually forms a circle.

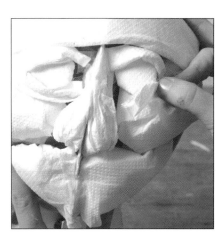

10 This will be the iris of the eye. Make a second iris in the same way. Now roll up some tissue paper and use it to shape each eye and hold in the iris. Stick the eyes in place.

portrait

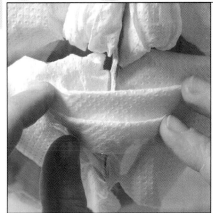

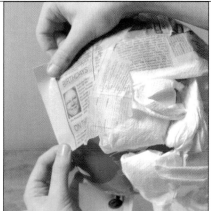

11 Fold some more paper into a mouth shape, ensuring that there is a defined line where the lips meet.

12 In a bowl, make up the glue solution as described (see page 47). Place strips of torn-up newspaper into the bowl and then leave them to soften for at least ten minutes to ensure that they are easy to blend.

13 Take a strip of newspaper and begin to build up your first layer of papier-mâché, taking care to cover the entire surface of the balloon, especially under the chin and around the back of the head.

14 When working on the eye and mouth areas, use smaller strips of newspaper to ensure that you do not cover up the lines of detail.

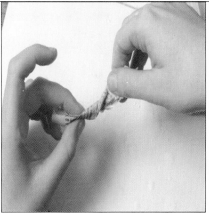

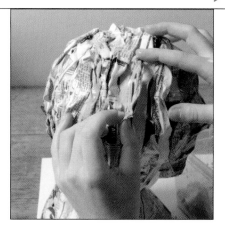

15 Continue to cover the head and neck until it is about five layers thick.

16 Twist long strips of newspaper to produce sections of papier-mâché hair that reflect the texture and styling of your subject's hair.

17 Build up the layers of hair until you are satisfied with the result.

18 Then leave the sculpture to dry, either overnight or in a warm place.

portrait

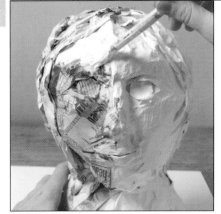

19 When your sculpture is completely dry, paint a white base coat all over it, taking care to work the paint into all of the gaps within the hair. Then leave the paint to dry.

20 When the base coat is dry, mix up a skin tone using white, red and yellow paint. Compare, and then alter, your colour to match your subject's skin tone before painting all of the skin areas of your sculpture.

21 Before these areas of paint have completely dried, mix a little blue paint into your skin colour and then paint the new shade onto the naturally shaded areas of the head, such as the eye sockets, cheekbones, chin and nose.

22 Add some more blue and a touch of black to your paint mixture and then paint in the nostrils, eyelashes, eyebrows and lip line. Now mix the iris colour and finish painting the eyes.

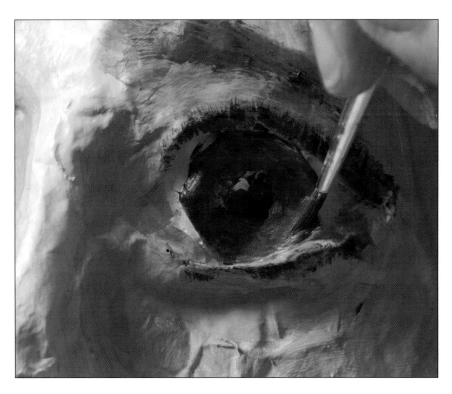

23 Mix up a shade of paint that matches your subject's hair colour and then paint the hair.

24 You can make your portrait as true to life, or as exaggerated, as you wish.

diving woman

Clay-modelling follows one of two methods: either modelling through joining slabs of clay or, as we will discover in this project, modelling the clay by pulling it out of a single block. Although this method requires more consideration and exploration of the clay, it is a very safe and strong way of working because the sculpture will have no weak points as a result of joining slabs of clay. When modelling in this way, you press into the clay, simultaneously producing a hollow and a protruding area: when pressing into the eye sockets, for instance, you'll create the hollow sockets at the same time as the protruding nose.

The uncomplicated form that I have chosen for this project – a diving, rotund woman – will lend itself very well to this way of working, as well as bringing some humour to your work. Because it is a great way of instantly connecting with the viewer, in the same way that we laugh when a comedian points out our human flaws, humour can be an important element in sculpture. Indeed, some of the most famous artists have observed and commented on the absurdities and ironies of life, along with social interactions, through sculpture. To accentuate the humorous character of this sculpture, we shall use a bright, colourful paint finish that parodies traditional ornamentation.

We will be making further use of our diving woman later on in the book as the object that we shall cast using a latex solution (see pages 75 to 79).

woman

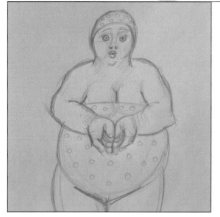

1 It is always important to start any figurative project by either sketching or studying the human form in photographs. Having done this, I have designed a caricature of a rotund, diving woman.

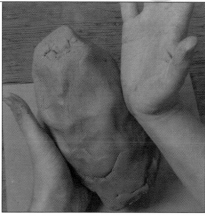

2 Take a large lump – about four fistfuls – from a fresh bag of clay and form a rough cylindrical shape.

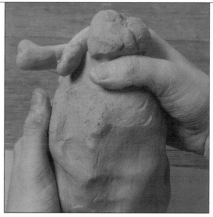

3 Working at the top of the cylinder, start to pull the clay to form a rough head, squeezing around where the neck will be.

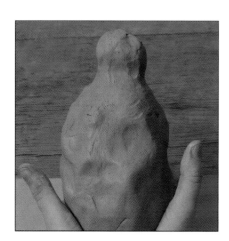

4 At the bottom of the cylinder, squeeze the clay to form the lower-leg and ankle area.

5 Just above the halfway point, ease out the clay a little to form a point (this will eventually be the woman's pointing hands as she prepares to dive).

6 Begin shaping the arms by developing the pointed area, easing out the elbows and starting to form the shoulders.

7 Using a knife, add definition to the arms and neck area by pushing the clay into shape.

8 Use your fingers to define her bottom.

9 Again using a knife, model the woman's breasts.

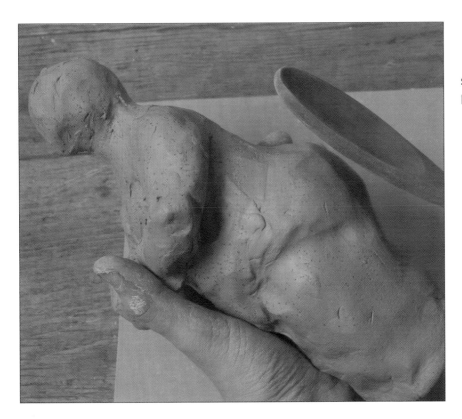

10 Using a wooden spoon, gently tap the woman's stomach and bottom to produce a curvy form.

woman

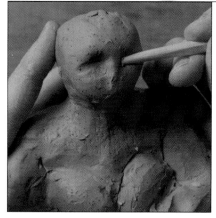

11 Now that the body is almost finished, it is time to concentrate on creating the face. First press a small knife or flat tool into the clay to form the eye sockets and nose. Then poke holes in the eye sockets with a pointed tool. Now create the eyes by filling the holes with two rolled-up balls of clay.

12 Using the small knife or flat tool, now press down on either side of the nose to create the cheeks.

13 Then press down under the nose to create the top lip.

14 Press below the top lip to create the lower lip and chin.

15 Now we will move on to the hands. First use a flat tool to create the basic planes that make up the pointing hands.

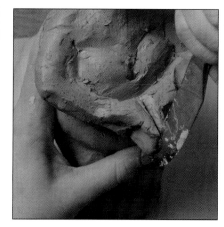

16 Using a knife, divide the planes into two separate hands.

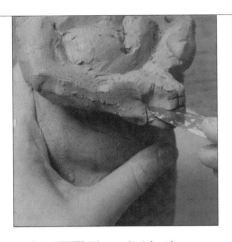

17 Then divide the hands into individual fingers and thumbs.

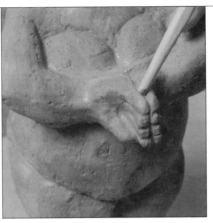

18 Using a pointed tool, define the fingers and thumbs and finish off the hands.

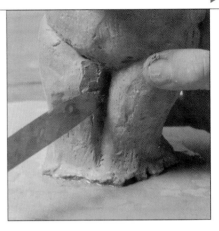

19 Using a flat tool, press and scrape the legs into shape.

20 Use a pointed tool to define all the details.

21 Leave the model to dry before hollowing it out by scooping out clay from the back and then covering the hole (as described on page 30).

22 When it is completely dry, paint a base coat of white paint over the figure.

woman

23 When this is dry, mix up a flesh tone and paint the body area.

24 Take care while you are doing this, and use a small brush when painting the facial features.

25 Decide on the colour and design of the woman's swimwear (I have chosen a blue base with paler-blue dots), paint it on and then leave the paint to dry.

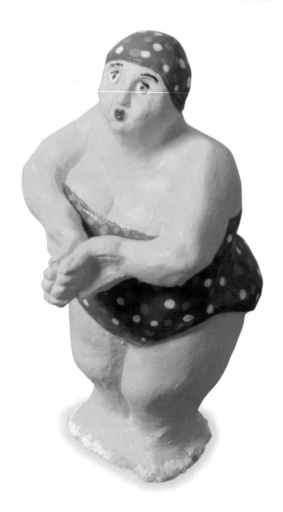

26 When your diving woman is dry, display her by standing her in a pile of sand, which will make her appear as though she is about to dive into the sea.

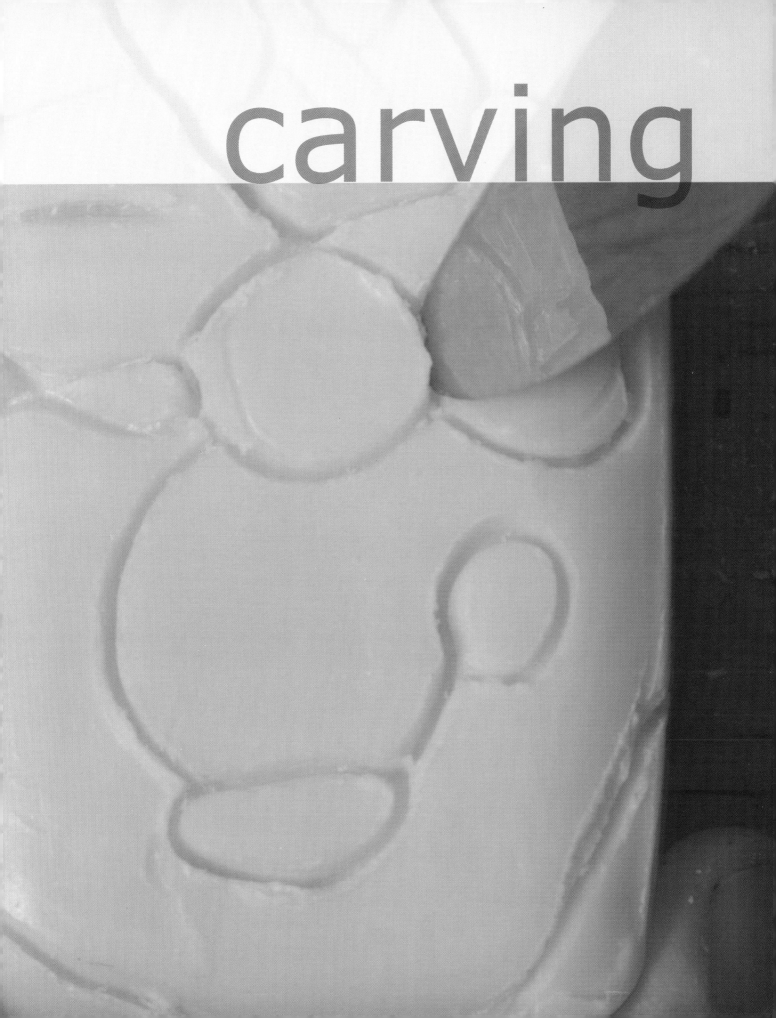

carving

relief-cast memory box ▶▶

you will need

a selection of found objects.
  two 30 cm (11 in) lengths
  of 10.25 x 2.5 cm (4 x 1 in)
  wood
two 20 cm (8 in) lengths of
  10.25 x 2.5 cm (4 x 1 in) wood
a drill
eight screws
a screwdriver
two roller guides measuring
  6 cm (about 2 in) in depth
a rolling pin
clay
clingfilm
plaster and a plastic bowl
a pin
a hard brush,
  such as a toothbrush
paintbrushes
black and white acrylic paint.
silver paint powder

Relief-carving is an age-old tradition, and we will emulate this style using a relief-casting method. Relief-casting is essentially the principle of creating an indentation and then filling the indentation with plaster to create a replica of the original object. Because there are never any undercuts or hollows and the cast is always easily removed, this method does not need the complex segmentations that some types of casting require.

For our subject, we will use a form of self-portraiture. There are many ways of approaching a memory box: one is to include a selection of 'found objects' that reflect your personality, such as pencils if you draw, your favourite pieces of jewellery, sports equipment, sweets, coins from countries that you have visited or any other objects that have particular significance for you. I have chosen some of my favourite pieces of jewellery, a tennis ball, some pencils, a crystal doorknob and a gold pebble, all of which reflect my interests and the things that are important to me. You could also create a memory box for a loved one or for a young relative, perhaps containing a teething ring, rattle, first tooth or toy, to treasure when they are older. An alternative option is to produce a tactile composition by selecting objects that have interesting surface textures.

The finish that we shall be using gives the impression of being a pewter cast. Because bronze, pewter and precious metals are very expensive to use, as well as requiring expert help and facilities, we will instead emulate a metal cast, albeit one that looks very real and creates a greater sense of importance. If you like the pewter effect, you could experiment with other metallic effects, such as gold and bronze, simply by changing the colour of the paint that you apply.

box

1 Gather together a group of objects that have both interesting surfaces and represent you in some way. You won't break these objects or make them dirty, but they must be fairly hard if they are to produce a clear imprint.

2 If you haven't already done so, cut two pieces of 10.25 x 2.5 cm (4 x 1 in) wood to a length of approximately 30 cm (11 in). Then cut another two pieces to a length of 20 cm (8 in). These will form the rectangle into which you will cast your plaster. (You may need to vary the size of the frame so that it holds all of your items.)

3 Drill two holes into both ends of the shorter pieces of wood and then screw the frame together.

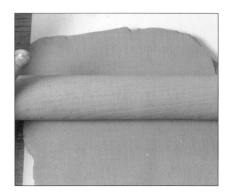

4 Using two roller guides 6 cm (about 2 in) deep and a rolling pin, roll out a slab of clay so that it is larger than the outside of the frame.

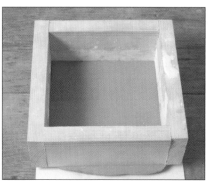

5 Push the frame into the clay. (This will stop the plaster from leaking out when you pour it into the frame.)

6 Spread a sheet of clingfilm over the surface of the clay. Now spend some time flattening any creases on the surface to ensure that your objects do not become dirty or damaged when you push them into the clay.

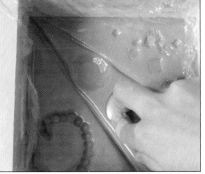

7 Arrange your objects on the clingfilm, experimenting with different compositions until you are happy with your design.

8 Taking one object at a time, push each firmly into the clay, taking care not to wiggle them around and thus distort the indentation's definition. Then carefully remove each object.

9 Peel back the clingfilm to reveal your relief composition. If you are not happy with it, roll out the clay again and then compose it differently.

10 Mix up a bowl of plaster (see page 15), ensuring that you squeeze out all of the lumps. Then tap the bowl to release any air bubbles.

box

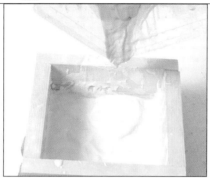

11 Take a little plaster in your hand and flick it onto the surface of the clay. (This not only prevents air bubbles from forming, but also helps to pick up all of the details.)

12 When you have flicked on a complete layer of plaster, slowly pour in the rest. Tap the sides of the frame to release any trapped air bubbles and prick them with a pin when they rise to the surface.

13 Leave the plaster to set until it has become hard and cold. It is important to leave the plaster until it has fully set because you may otherwise break the plaster cast when you remove it from the mould.

14 When the plaster is completely dry, unscrew the short ends of the frame and gently tap the sides to release the frame from the plaster. Ease off the frame so that you are left with the plaster cast and the clay. Peel back the clay, which will still be wet. (You could probably use it again to make another cast.)

15 You now have a finished plaster relief plaque.

16 Hold the plaque under running water. Then use a brush or toothbrush to clean it up, taking care to get the clay out of all of the detailed crevices. Leave the plaque, which will have absorbed some water, to dry.

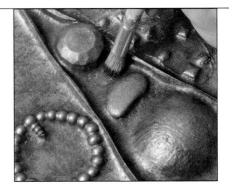

17 Paint the entire plaque – front, back and sides – with black acrylic paint.

18 In a bowl, add a little white to the black paint to make a dark-grey colour. Dip a stubby paintbrush into the paint, dab off the excess so that the brush is quite dry and then stipple the grey paint all over the surface of the plaque.

19 Clean and dry the stubby brush, dip it into some silver powder and then stipple the powder all over the surface of the plaque, building up a stronger layer on the areas that are raised the highest. This will produce a burnished effect.

20 Now leave the plaque to dry. When it is completely dry, you could display it on a decorative plate stand.

soap sculpture

you will need

a bar of soap

clay-carving tools,
including a knife and
a pointed tool

In this project we will use a simple and familiar material to create a carving in the style of the prehistoric Maori carvings found in New Zealand. I have researched various museum collections and have produced several drawings to enable you to create your own version of one of these traditional, symbolic carvings. These sculptures were often used in fertility rituals (which is why the breasts and stomach are typically prominent), and similar carvings were often worn as talismans, either to protect the wearer from evil spirits or to bring him or her strength or good fortune. I have combined all of the key characteristics of these carvings in my design, which you can either follow or use as inspiration to design your own following the steps as a guide.

Carving is one of the hardest methods of sculpture creation, but you will find a bar of soap much more manageable than stone (it won't chip), as well as much less expensive (the cheapest soap will do), so that any mistakes that you may make will not be costly and you can also easily start again. You will need at least a couple of carving tools: a knife with which to cut away the outside of the soap and a pointed tool, such as a skewer, with which to create holes and finishing details.

sculpture

1 Either design your own talisman after looking at prehistoric Maori sculptures or follow my design.

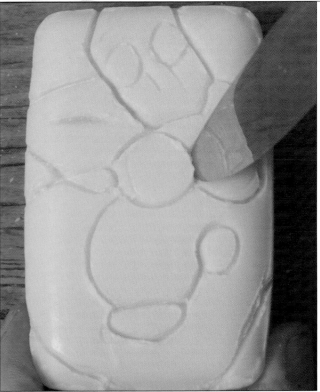

3 Once you have lightly etched the design onto the soap, use the pointed tool to make the incision deeper so that you can clearly see the outline and detail of your design.

2 Using a pointed tool, lightly draw the design onto the bar of soap, working right to the edges. It may take you a couple of attempts to get it right, and remember that if you draw lightly enough, any mistakes won't be a problem.

4 Using a knife, carefully scrape and shape the sculpture's outside edge. Do this very carefully because if you try to remove too much at once, the soap may break off irregularly.

5 Using the pointed tool, gouge out the holes that define the design's arms and legs. Again be careful not to take off too much soap in case you break off the arm or leg section.

6 Use the knife to scrape away some of the arms' and legs' surfaces. This will raise the head and body areas to give a more three-dimensional effect.

7 Now that the breasts are higher than the legs and arms, begin to shape them to make them more spherical. Shape the stomach, as you did the breasts, to make it more spherical.

sculpture

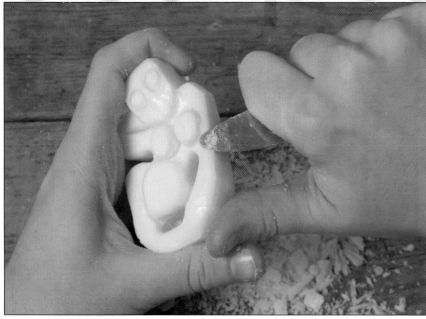

8 Now that the basic shape has been formed, start to shape and soften the sculpture as a whole, smoothing the corners and graduating the holes.

9 Use the pointed tool to add extra definition to the lines on the carving, making sure that the lines around the eyes are particularly deep.

10 The finished piece.

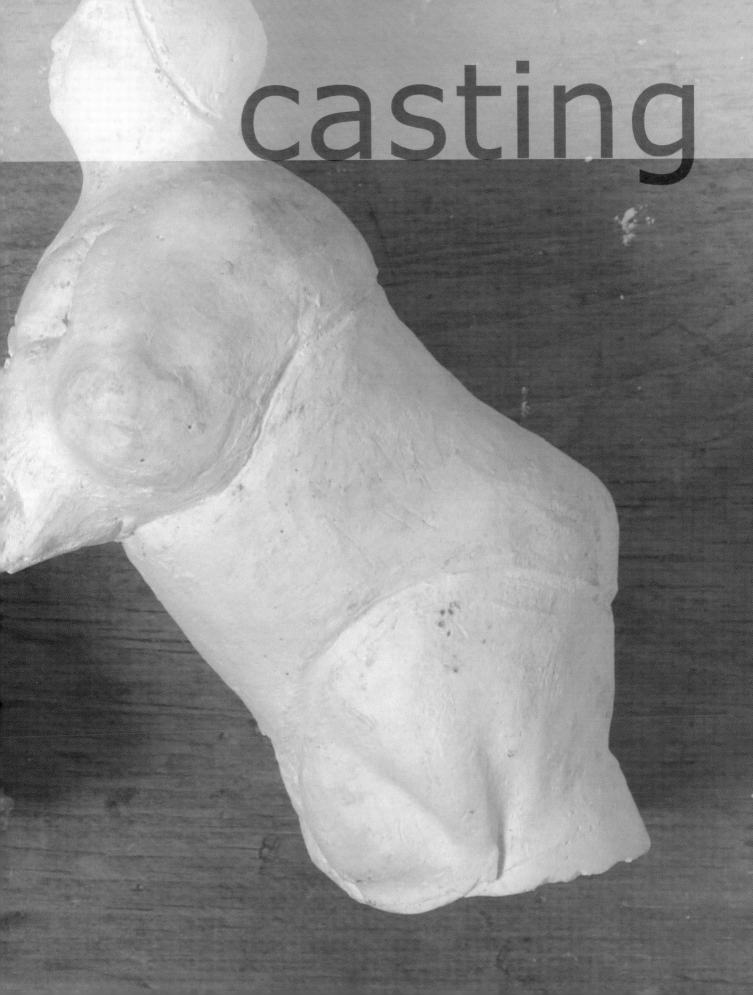

casting

diving-women casts ▶▶

you will need

a finished diving-woman
    sculpture (see pages 55 to 60)

latex

three containers/jars

an old, medium-sized paintbrush

a pointed tool

scissors

sticky tape

soft fabric

plaster, water and a plastic bowl

sandpaper

ready-mixed plaster

neutral-coloured shoe polish

a shallow metal dish

Our first project using the casting method requires you to make an unpainted diving woman (see pages 55 to 60) from clay. The casting medium will be latex, and we'll be building up a rubber coating that picks up all of the subject's surface details, as well as creating a flexible mould that can easily be removed and reused. Another benefit of casting with latex is that you can vary the strength of the mould so that it is either tight or stretchy, enabling you to achieve some very interesting distortion effects.

One of the main difficulties with casting is planning segmentations in the mould to enable you to lift it off the cast object easily without it becoming stuck in any recesses or undercuts. This is not a problem when working with latex, however, because latex stretches without breaking when it is removed and then reforms itself. This flexibility means that when you fill the mould with plaster, the latex may stretch and expand, causing slight distortions in the structure of the form. We will use the distortional properties of latex to our advantage in this project: because it has few undercuts, the diving-woman form that we will be using will become evenly distorted, actually adding to her bulging figure.

This project will also teach you to display your sculpture inventively, with particular reference to the tradition of water sculpture, as exemplified by Italian baroque fountains and many more contemporary public sculptures found in a number of cities.

When painting on latex, make sure that your working area is well ventilated. Keep your latex in an airtight container because it dries very quickly when it comes into contact with the air. Always use an old brush because the latex will dry onto it, making it useless.

women

1 Wait until your clay model of the diving woman (see pages 55 to 60) is completely dry before beginning this project. You can do this at the unpainted stage if you prefer.

2 Pour a small amount of latex into a container (because latex dries very quickly, doing this will ensure that the bulk of it won't be spoiled).

3 Using an old, medium-sized paintbrush, start applying latex to the head, making sure that you fill in all of the facial crevices.

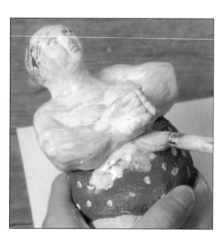

4 Paint the rest of the body, taking care to cover all of the hard-to-see areas like under the arms and hands.

5 Repeat steps 3 and 4 until the latex has dried to become a dark-yellow or orange colour. (You'll probably need to apply about ten coats.)

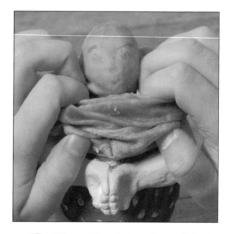

6 When the latex has dried completely, carefully begin to peel back the mould. Although the mould will be fairly stretchy, you will have to tug quite hard to pull it over the hands. The mould will then be inside out.

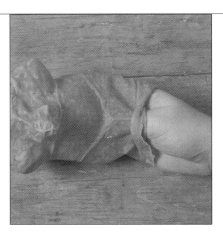

7 Turn the mould outside in and then rinse it under running water to remove any clay dust.

8 Cut off the bottom of a plastic bottle or cup to create a mini-dish.

9 Using a pointed tool, skewer a hole in the centre of the dish and then cut into and around it with a pair of scissors to make a large hole.

10 Fit the plastic dish into the base of the mould and then tape the mould to the dish (we'll be pouring plaster into the mould at this point).

11 Edge the rim of another plastic container with some soft, bunched-up fabric. (The cup will support the model as the plaster dries out, while the fabric will ensure that the cup does not create an indentation in the model.)

12 Mix up a bowl of plaster (see page 15 for instructions), taking care to squeeze out all of the lumps. Then tap the bowl to encourage the air bubbles to rise to the surface.

women

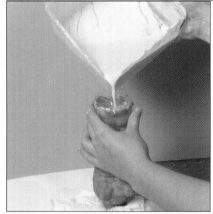

13 Holding the mould above the cup, pour the plaster into the mould. When the mould is full, tap it from all sides to encourage any air bubbles that would otherwise create holes in the finished cast to rise to the surface.

14 Hold the mould for a couple of minutes until the plaster starts to become firm, then carefully lower the head end into the padded plastic cup until the model ends up resting on its shoulders. Leave the plaster to dry (this make take a few hours).

15 When the plaster is dry, peel back the latex. You will find that the woman's shape is slightly rounder than in the original version, but this is part of the effect.

16 Using the same mould, repeat the casting and finishing processes (steps 11 to 15) twice more so that you end up with three diving women.

17 When all of the casts are completely dry, rub some neutral-coloured wax or shoe polish over each one's surface (this will make the plaster appear more stone-like).

18 If you want to add some more detail, use a darker polish to create a rather 'granite-like' effect on protruding parts.

19 You may have other ideas about how best to display your figures, but I have decided to create an interesting display using water. I have placed the figures, facing outwards, in the centre of a ceramic pot and have then filled the pot with water to create a sculptural water feature.

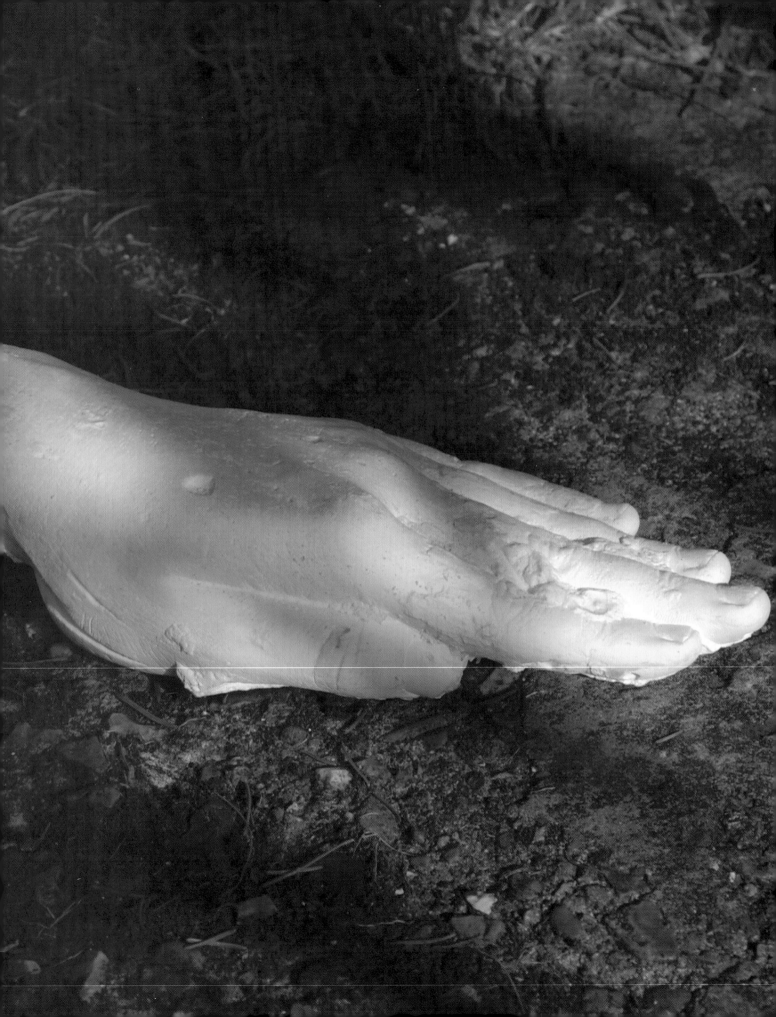

arm cast

you will need

clay

a rolling pin

two roller guides

petroleum jelly or vegetable oil

plaster and a plastic bowl

coloured paint (I've used pink)

a pile of fabric

a chisel and a mallet

a scrubbing brush

neutral-coloured shoe polish

   or wax

a cloth

The white-marble, figurative sculptures of ancient Greece are some of the most hauntingly beautiful works of art ever produced, the qualities with which each figure is imbued giving a sense of grace, purity and dynamism. How we view these relics is, however, very different to how they would have been perceived when they were first created because although they are now white all over, they would actually have been so brightly painted that we would probably consider them garish today. Another characteristic that adds to their beauty is that although many of these sculptures are broken, often missing arms, legs and sometimes heads, their ruined state is somehow poetic, leaving room for your imagination to rebuild what has been lost.

In this project, we will use a casting method that involves a degree of carving to produce a similar 'relic'. This method enables undercuts and hollows to be cast without having to devise a complicated segment cast. We will make a mould and cast plaster into it, and when it is dry, we will chip away at the outer mould to reveal the sculpture within. Because you will see how a form unfolds from a lump of plaster, the process of chipping away the mould is a good way of understanding the carving process.

You may wish to carve out the whole arm or to leave part of the arm bound in the mould, as if it were an unfinished carving. You could use either your own arm as a model (although this may prove slightly tricky unless you're well prepared) or make a cast of a friend or family member's arm. If you opt for the latter, not only will you enjoy working together, but you'll also create a lasting memory of that person.

cast

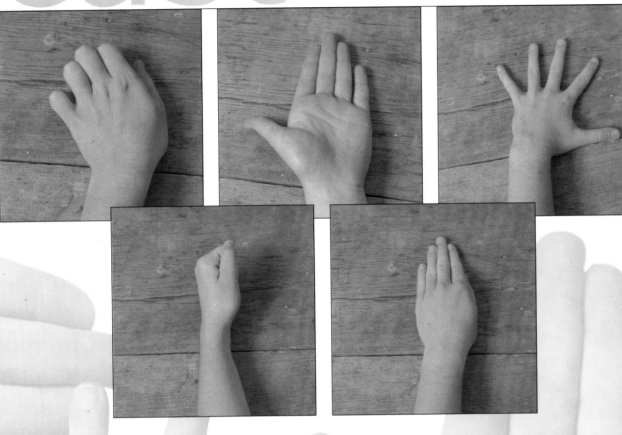

1 First decide how you want to position the arm. (If this is your first attempt, I'd recommend a simple position with not too many undercuts.)

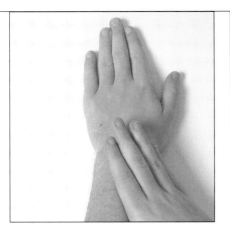

2 Thoroughly smear some petroleum jelly or vegetable oil all around the arm. (This will stop the plaster from sticking to the skin and will prevent you from ripping out any hairs.)

3 Mix up half a bowl of plaster (see page 15).

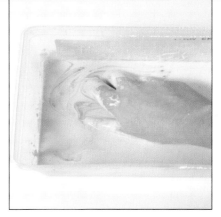

4 Then add a few drops of coloured paint – I've used pink – so that the plaster is noticeably coloured. (When you begin to chip away the mould later on, the colour will let you know that you are nearing the cast and that you should therefore work carefully.)

5 Flick small amounts of plaster onto the surface of the arm

6 Mix up another batch of plaster (there's no need to colour this batch).

7 Then spread it over the coloured layer.

cast

8 Continue to build up layers of plaster until you've created a mould that is about 3 cm (1 in) thick.

9 Then leave the plaster to dry until it has become solid enough to remove without breaking it (it does not have to be cold and dry).

10 When the mould is dry, turn it over, using clay to hold it in place.

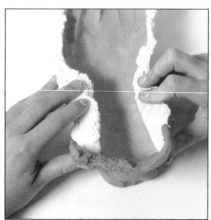

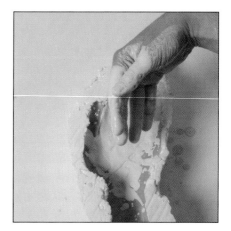

11 Now rub some petroleum jelly or vegetable oil over the inside of the mould to prevent the plaster from sticking to itself when you cast it.

12 Build up a clay wall around the open end of the mould to stop the plaster from running out when you pour it in.

13 Mix up a bowl of plaster, squeeze out the lumps and then tap the sides of the bowl to release any air bubbles. Now flick a layer of plaster over the surface of the mould.

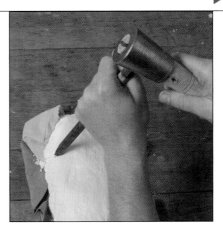

▶ ▶

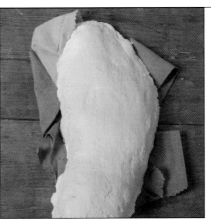

14 Pour the rest of the plaster into the mould. Then tap the sides of the mould and pop any air bubbles before leaving the cast to dry thoroughly (the dryer it is, the easier chipping off the mould will be).

15 When the cast has dried, take off the clay and place the mould on a pile of newspapers or fabric (this will ensure that the fabric takes the pressure, not the cast, when you're chipping off the plaster).

16 Using a chisel and mallet, begin carefully to chip away at the plaster mould. (You may, however, find it easier to use a variety of tools that gouge or lever off the plaster.) The plaster will break away in chunks, which you should clear away as you work.

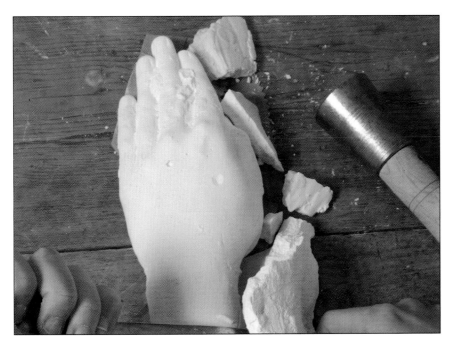

17 Take extra care when you reach the pink layer because the plaster will come away from the cast cleanly, and you will not have to hit it very hard. You may have to use a small knife to lever off the clay that remains stuck in the smaller gaps and details.

cast

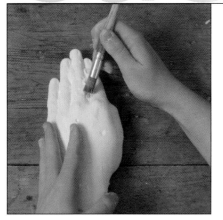

18 When you have chipped away all of the mould, scrub what residue you can off the cast of the arm with a brush, then rinse under a running tap. Then leave it to dry out thoroughly.

19 When the plaster arm is dry, create an aged effect by rubbing in some neutral-coloured shoe polish or wax with a cloth.

20 When waxed, buff with a cloth.

21 The finished piece.

metal mobile

you will need

wire cutters
   (or a pair of strong scissors)
wire pincers
a roll of metal wire
silver spray paint
a pencil
a piece of card measuring
   3 x 56cm (1 x 22 in.)
a pair of scissors
a piece of sheet metal
a marker pen
metal file
a hammer and nail

As a result of the advances in technology using motors and airstreams, kinetic art, which makes literal movement an aspect of sculpture, has become increasingly popular. Indeed, kinetic art has often developed in close association with science, and many laboratories and universities offer residencies to enable artists to create work in response to the field of science in which they are interested. Rather than capturing the effects of movement that we have explored in previous projects, kinetic art relies on movement to complete the sculpture. Using electric motors and elaborate clockwork circuits, the artist can either direct the movement or take inspiration from the intervention of the natural airflows and movements around the piece. There is a strong sense of the fantastic in many kinetic sculptures, particularly the work of Alexander Calder (1898–1976), who created mobiles from brightly coloured pieces of metal suspended from metal rods.

In this project, we will use the format of the mobile as the basis for producing a kinetic sculpture. Sonic art is a developing area of art practice that uses sounds and tones to produce transient experiences that are neither music nor conventional art, and our sculpture will not only move, but will also produce sounds as the metal elements knock together in the air.

We will be using sheet metal and metal wire to produce our sculpture. It is not important which type of metal you use, as long as you are able to cut it into the desired shapes. If your sheet metal is thin enough (1 or 2 mm or 1/16 in), you may be able to cut it with a pair of strong kitchen scissors; alternatively, you may prefer to buy some metal cutters or a special pair of scissors.

mobile

1 Using wire cutters or a pair of strong scissors, cut two lengths of metal wire measuring 60 cm (about 23 in), four lengths measuring 40 cm (15 in) and eight lengths measuring 30 cm (11 in). Divide the lengths into two groups, so that each group consists of one length of wire measuring 60 cm (23 in), two measuring 40 cm (15 in) and four measuring 30 cm (11 in). We will call these two groups 'A' and 'B'.

2 Take the 60 cm (23 in) length of wire from group A and bend it in the middle to make a hook from which you can suspend the mobile.

3 Now bend the ends of the wire from the middle to create an upturned 'V' shape.

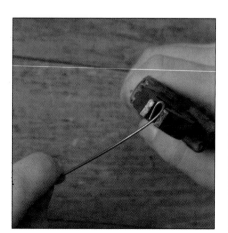

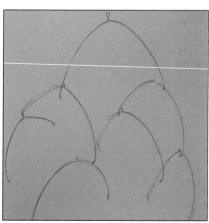

4 Using wire pincers, curl round the ends of the 'V' to create hooks that will hold the next layer of the mobile.

5 Bend all of the other lengths of wire in group A in the same way. Hook all the 'V' shapes together to make a finished side.

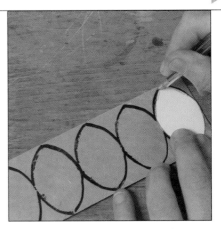

6 You should find that the layers all join together, so that the hooks at the ends of the 60 cm (23 in) length connect with the 40 cm (15 in) lengths and the hooks of those connect with the 30 cm (11 in) lengths. Link the mobile's components firmly together by tightly closing the hooks around the top of the upturned 'V's. You have now have produced the first side (side A) of your kinetic sculpture. Repeat steps 2 to 6 with the lengths of wire in group B to form the second pyramidal side (side B) of your sculpture.

7 With a pencil, draw a leaf shape (or another simple shape) on a piece of card measuring about 3 x 6 cm (1 x 2 in). This will be the template for your metal shapes.

8 Cut out the shape with a pair of scissors, place it on the sheet metal and draw around it with a marker pen. Create sixteen outlines in this way.

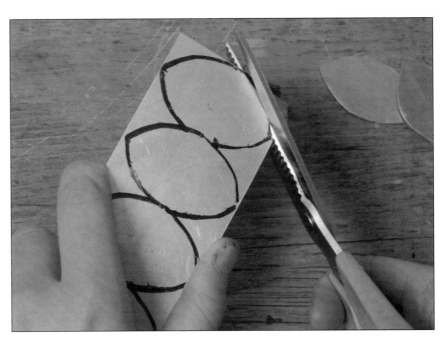

9 Using wire cutters or a pair of strong scissors, cut out all of the leaf shapes. (This will be quite hard work and it may be advisable to protect your hands by wearing a pair of gloves.)

mobile

10 The edges of each metal shape will be sharp, so the next step is to sand them down with a file.

11 Gently hammer one side of the first leaf. This will produce an interesting surface pattern and will also cause the metal to curl upwards a little, rather like a leaf. Hammer the remaining fifteen shapes in this way, too.

12 Using a hammer and a punch or nail, hammer a hole through the top of each leaf.

13 Using wire pincers, pull the mobile's wire hooks through the holes in the leaves so that every hook at the bottom of the structure has a leaf attached to it.

14 Hang up one side to free your hands and then place side B over side A to make a cross shape when viewed from above.

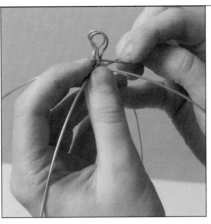

15 Cut a short length of wire and then bind the two sides together around the top of the first hook.

16 Hang each side of the sculpture in a well-ventilated area and spray it with silver spray paint. When the paint is dry, spray on a second coat and then put the halves to one side.

17 Spray each half of the mobile with a final coat of silver paint. When it is dry, hang it from its top hook in an area that people often pass through to encourage it to move and tinkle in an airstream.

architectural scape

A4-sized photocopies of
architectural drawings
and photographs
pair of scissors
glue/glue gun
eight pieces of card,
sized to fit your design
a paintbrush
a selection of paints with
which to produce the colours
red, orange, yellow, green,
turquoise, blue and purple.

Architecture and sculpture enjoy a very special relationship because they are the only creative disciplines that work with real space, by which I mean that they do not produce illusions of space as painting and printing do. Architecture has always formed a key part of most artistic movements, such as expressionism and modernism, as well as defining the 'look' of each period of history. Architecture provides us with structures in which to live, and sometimes also a lifestyle, while sculpture is often designed as a complement to, and an extension of, a specific building in order to illuminate and intensify the architect's design.

This project will give you the opportunity to look at many different styles of architecture and will help you to learn to recognise the sculptural elements and principles within them. Before beginning this project, take the time to look through books that contain photographs of various styles and types of building. Then make photocopies of any images that strike you as being particularly interesting and try to photocopy a variety of detailed structures that perhaps include columns, carved details and larger features like balconies or domes.

So far our projects have presented sculpture as a three-dimensional medium that considers all views as part of the whole form. In this project, we will challenge this convention by creating a three-dimensional sculpture from two-dimensional elements. We will also use colour theory as a means of directing the eye through space, giving a greater sense of three-dimensional space by painting each element a colour of the rainbow and then positioning them in following progression: red, orange, yellow, green, turquoise, blue and purple, which then leads back to red again.

architectural

1 Earmark a variety of photographs and drawings of interesting buildings or architectural features, such as doors, windows or domes, to photocopy.

2 Photocopy all of these architectural images onto A4-sized paper.

3 Select your favourite features and then cut them out.

4 Look at the architectural elements that you have cut out and start to play around with them to create a composition that looks like a fantastic new building.

5 When you have decided on your final composition, stick its elements onto a piece of card.

6 Photocopy your design seven times and stick each copy onto a piece of card.

7 Working with each copy in turn, cut out the building, as well as any holes or windows in the design, which will add an interesting effect to the finished work.

8 When you have cut out all seven buildings, colour the whole of each in turn using a watery paint mixture in the colours listed above, so that you have a red building, an orange building and so on.

9 Using a strong glue, line the base edge of the bottom of your buildings.

10 Hold them in place while they dry. Remember to arrange the buildings in the correct colour order before gluing them.

11 For extra support, glue the buildings together where they join further up.

12 Your rainbow sculpture is now finished.

mirror triptych

▶ ▶

you will need

a piece of card about 2 to 3 mm
($\frac{1}{16}$ to $\frac{2}{16}$ in) thick

a pencil

a ruler

a pair of scissors

a knife

sticky tape

mirror card

glue/glue gun

a small wire hook

In this project, we will focus on the triptych sculptures of the medieval period that fused two-dimensional wall-paintings with three-dimensional relief sculptures. The format of the triptych consists of three panels of painting or sculpture that usually either narrate a biblical event, such as the Annunciation, or provide a scene for the artist's patron to contemplate when at worship. Triptychs often depict the mother-and-child theme, sometimes also incorporating a portrait of the patron of the piece.

In the previous project, we looked at the important relationship between sculpture and architecture. We will use this crossover format again, but this time concentrating on the crossover between painting and sculpture, to learn about wall-based sculpture, which teaches us that sculpture doesn't have to follow the conventional rules of three dimensions. (In fact, the different artistic mediums of sculpture, painting and printing – and even music, literature and performance – are increasingly coming together and drawing inspiration from each other.)

In this project, we will give the traditional subject and function of this style of work a contemporary twist. Although we will use the traditional structure of three separate panels, along with the concept of self-reflection and contemplation, instead of using figurative painting, we will use mirror card as our focus for meditation. We will be bending the mirror card to experiment with the concept of reflection and the contemplation of our self-image in the same way as we do at the fairground when we walk into a hall of mirrors and move around to produce different images of ourselves.

mirror

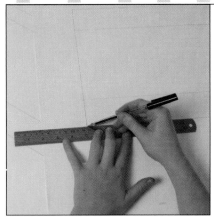

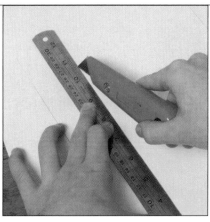

1 On a sheet of card about 2 to 3 mm ($\frac{1}{16}$ to $\frac{2}{16}$ in) thick, and using a pencil and ruler, draw two rectangles that measure 30 x 20 cm (11 x 8 in) and one rectangle that measures 30 x 25 cm (11 x 9 in). Taking the first two rectangles in turn, mark a 5 cm (2 in) strip running from the top of the 30 cm (11) side to the bottom of the other 30 cm (11) side. Then measure and mark a 5 cm (2 in) strip at both ends of the remaining rectangle, again running from the top to the bottom.

2 Cut out these shapes so that you have two rectangles with a 5 cm (2 in) strip at one end and one rectangle with a 5 cm (2 in) strip at each end.

3 Using a knife, lightly score downwards along the strips.

4 Then bend the strips along the scored lines so that they stand at right angles to the rectangles.

5 Position the three rectangles together so that you have (when viewed from left to right) a 5 cm (2 in) strip, a rectangle, a strip, a rectangle, a strip, a rectangle and, finally, a strip.

6 Tape together at the back to form your triptych's basic box shape.

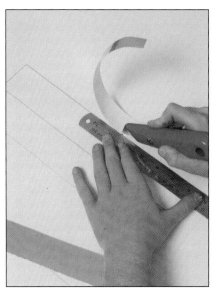

7 Turn over a sheet of mirror card so that the unmirrored side is uppermost (this will enable you to see your markings more clearly). Using a pencil and ruler, draw two rectangles measuring 30 x 5 cm (11 x 2 in) and two rectangles measuring 30 x 10 cm (11 x 4 in)

8 Cut out these rectangles.

mirror

9 Then score the 30 x 10 cm (11 x 4 in) rectangles in half lengthways.

10 Glue the smaller mirrored rectangles to the insides of the outer two strips of card that form the edges of the box. Fold and glue the larger rectangles to the inner strips that form the central divisions of the triptych.

11 Draw another three rectangles on the mirror card, this time measuring 40 x 15 cm (15 x 6 in). Now draw in strips measuring 2 cm (1 in) at the top and bottom of the 15 cm (6 in) sides.

12 Cut out these shapes and score along the 2 cm (1 in) strips. These rectangles will form the main panels of your triptych. Bend the 2 cm (1 in) strips.

13 Then tape them down to the back of the triptych so that the mirror-card panels curve outwards.

14 Take a little time to experiment with your mirror-card panels by pushing them down at different points to create various wave effects.

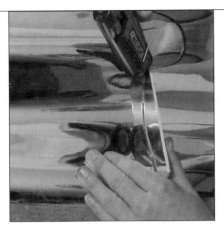

15 Working with each panel in turn, apply some glue in a horizontal strip from one side of the back of the panel to the other, push the mirror card down so that it forms a wavy panel and hold it in place until the glue has dried.

16 When the glue on all of the panels has dried, attach a small wire hook to the back of your triptych to enable you to hang it on a wall.

assemblage sculpture ▶▶

you will need

a selection of found objects

glue or other fixing agents

spray paint (colour optional)

a found object, such as a log
or bucket, to act as a plinth

Assemblage sculpture is concerned with choosing everyday, 'found objects' and then constructing them to create either an abstract sculpture that aims to produce an interesting composition or an imaginative figurative sculpture. Many sculptors work in this way, often to quite a large scale, using old railway sleepers, for example, or chains and ropes from boat yards and other industrial cast-offs.

Try to be completely open-minded when selecting your objects – which could be plastic cups, old pieces of metal, boxes, twigs and bark, fabric and trimmings or even dried pasta – and remember that you are looking for any shapes, forms or textures that interest you. In this project, we will be primarily concerned with form and texture, so there's no need to concern yourself with the quality or colour of your found objects because after you've assembled them you'll be covering the entire sculpture with a coat of spray paint, thereby placing the focus on texture and form.

This project will inspire you to appreciate every three-dimensional form for its sculptural properties and will help you to build up a form-and-texture library in your mind that you can access for your future work.

assemblage

1 The first step is to collect as many objects with interesting forms or textures as you can. Be they junk, natural materials or even dried food, look out for intriguing objects wherever you go, whether it be the beach, a wood, a junkyard or your attic.

2 Lay out all of your objects in front of you and then start moving them around and placing objects with different textures side by side. Decide which textures, such as rough and smooth or hard and soft, work the most effectively together.

3 Now decide which forms or shapes, such as geometric and organic or large and small, complement each other best. This exercise will help you to design your composition.

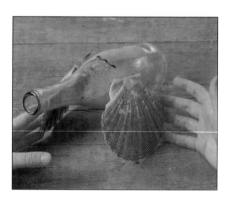

4 You must now decide on your main structure. You could create something dynamic, with lots of diagonal lines, or else a still composition whose curved and straight lines create a symmetrical, flowing effect.

5 Once you have settled on your design, glue or fix some of your larger structural found objects together to make the basic armature.

6 Take a moment to study the form that you have created. When sculpting in this way, it is very important to be in a state of constant 'conversation' with your sculpture, by which I mean that you should keep looking at, and studying, its strengths and weaknesses.

▶ ▶

7 When you are happy with the basic structure, review the textural objects that you collected and decide whether they will add anything to the surface of your sculpture.

8 As in step 5, you must now decide whether to make a feature of your textural objects' fixings.

9 Decide, too, whether to use contrasting or complementary textures. Remember that it is important to be consistent in your choices.

10 When you have completed your composition, wait for the glue to dry (if you have used it) before spray-painting your sculpture in an appropriate colour: a vibrant red for a dynamic composition, for example, or a passive blue for a still composition.

conclusion

Now that you have reached the end of the book, I hope that you have a clearer understanding of the many techniques, materials and approaches that constitute the medium of sculpture. As you embark on further projects of your own, the most important thing to remember is that there are no rules when creating artwork. You can make a sculpture from anything, with anything and about anything. You'll find inspiration all around you in every three-dimensional form, be it a tree, an animal, a building or even rubbish! You can also use sculpture to express your feelings or to investigate any ideas in which you are interested.

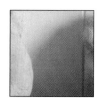
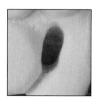

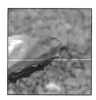

In my own work, I usually begin a project when I have been inspired by something that I have read or by an issue that I have been thinking about. I then consider how I can translate this idea into the medium of sculpture, taking care to choose materials that reflect the emotion or idea that I am trying to express. As an artist, I have worked in many different media (included here is a 'gallery' of my work that demonstrates the diversity of materials and approaches that constitute sculpture), and in the course of my art practice I draw, carve, construct, cast, model, paint, print, photograph and even act and sing! I hope that as a sculptor you will see that sculpture can be anything, and that it is important never to close your mind to new techniques, materials or approaches.

I hope, too, that this book has been an informative guide to the basic techniques and principles of sculpture, and that you will enjoy making and developing the projects in it. Good luck!

glossary

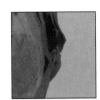

Abstract: when a subject is edited and reduced until it bears no direct visual likeness to the original subject.

Aesthetic: the style and emotional essence of the sculpture.

Armature: the basic skeletal structure of a sculpture, often a hidden support.

Complementary: when two similar forms, textures or colours, such as circular and oval, curly and wavy or blue and green, are placed next to each other.

Contrasting: when two opposite forms, textures or colours, such as rigid and floppy, rough and smooth or black and white, are placed next to each other.

Conversation: the questioning of your sculpture, for example, is it too large, too detailed or too colourful?

Dynamic: the capturing of movement using diagonal lines, vibrant, warm colours and detailed textures.

Figurative: when a sculpture represents, and bears a likeness to, its subject.

Form: an object or shape.

Passive: the capturing of stillness using symmetrical lines, pale, cool colours and smooth textures.

Plinth: the traditional presentation stand or block on which a sculpture may sit.

Sculptural language: a visual understanding and articulation.

Structure: the strongest defining lines or shape of the form.

index

credits

I would like to dedicate this book to my mother – and best friend – for her unending support of all my artistic endeavours, and for sacrificing her kitchen table to my sculpting for the last ten years!

I would also like to thank my friends for their support and encouragement, especially Laura and Nic.

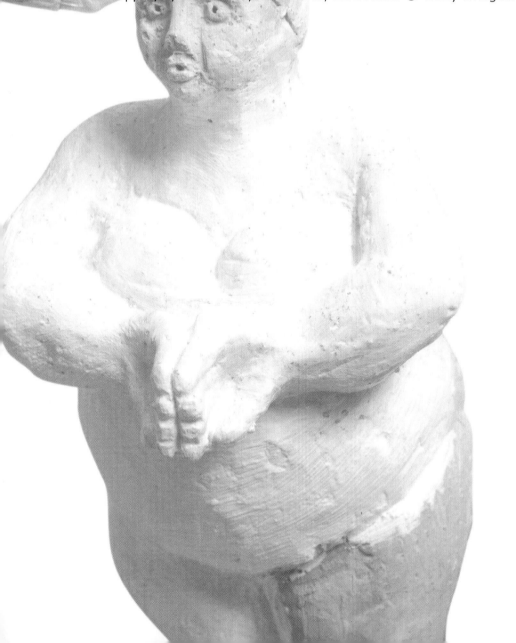